BASS
RECORDED VERSIONS
AUTHENTIC TRANSCRIPTIONS WITH NOTES AND TABLATURE

TRANSCRIBED BY STEVE GORENBERG

PEARL JAM ten

This publication is not for sale in the EC and/or Australia or New Zealand.

Due to contractural restrictions, the lyrics to "Release" cannot be reprinted in this book.

ISBN 0-7935-2368-0

HAL•LEONARD® CORPORATION
7777 W. BLUEMOUND RD. P.O. BOX 13819 MILWAUKEE, WI 53213

Copyright © 1993 by HAL LEONARD PUBLISHING CORPORATION
International Copyright Secured   All Rights Reserved

For all works contained herein:
Unauthorized copying, arranging, adapting, recording or public performance is an infringement of copyright.
Infringers are liable under the law.

it's kind of funny to have a book like this out when none of us have ever written our music out in this manner... that's not to say it's wrong; after all, there's no right or wrong in music... but if you are using this book, please interpret it in your own style... change the key... play it on a stand-up or a five string or through a fuzz box... and, when you've almost figured it out, close your eyes and use your ears — the direct line between your instrument and soul. thanks.

jeff ament

PEARL JAM ten

CONTENTS

14   Alive

23   Black

45   Deep

9   Even Flow

40   Garden

27   Jeremy

32   Oceans

4   Once

35   Porch

48   Release

19   Why Go

53   NOTATION LEGEND

Once

Music by Stone Gossard
Lyric by Eddie Vedder

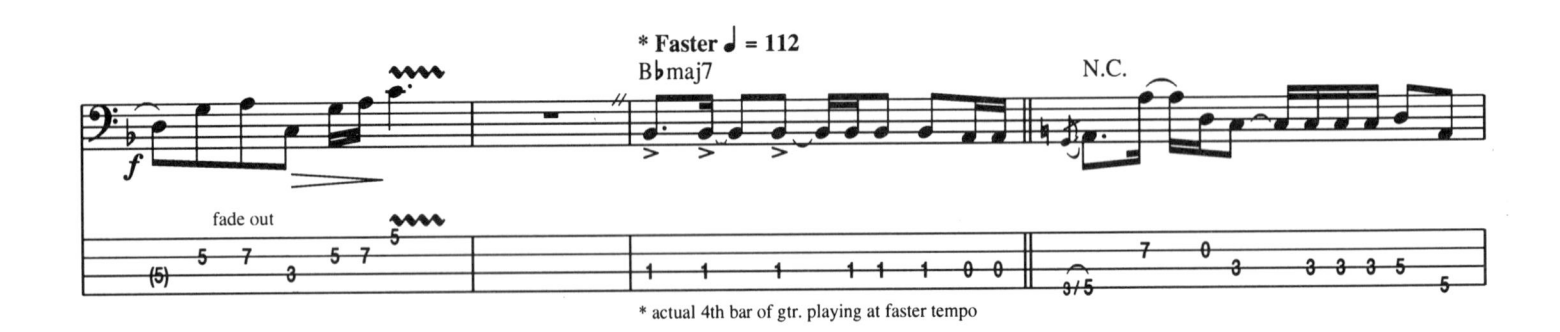

5

Bb5 C5 G5 A5 Bb5 C5
Oo, once up - on a time, I could
G5 D5
1.
Bb5
2.
Bb5
lose my - self, hey, hey. hey, hey, oh, ow!
Guitar Solo
A5 G5 A5 G5 A5 G5
A5 G5 A5 G5 A5 G5
A5 G5 Bb5
Interlude
N.C.

mf
Chorus
f
G5 A5 Bb5 C5
Oo. Once up - on a time, I could con -
G5 D5 Bb5 C5 G5 A5
trol my - self! Yeah! Once up - on a time,
Bb5 C5 G5 D5 Bb5 C5
I could lose my - self, hey, yeah, yeah, hey.
G5 A5 Bb5 C5
Once up - on a time, I could

G5 A5 Bb5 C5
love my - self!
Oo!
G5 A5 Bb5 C5 G5 A5
Once up - on a time, I could love you!
Bb5 C5 G5 A5 Bb5 C5
Yeah! Once! Once!
G5 A5 Bb5 C5 G5 A5
Once! Once! Yeah! Once!
Bb5 C5 G5 A5 Bb5 C5 G5
Once, hey, yeah! Yeah, hey yeah, yeah hey, hey, yeah, once!
let ring

Even Flow

Music by Stone Gossard
Lyric by Eddie Vedder

Ooh yeah. Whoa, hey now, faces that he sees come again ain't that familiar.
Oh, dealin', understands the weather or the winter's on its way.
Ooh yeah. Whoa, no grin he can't have when his happy looks insane. Ooh yeah.
Oh, ceilings few and far between all the legal hall of shame. Yeah.
To Coda 1
Chorus
D5
B♭5
E - ven - flow,
Fill 1
Harm.
(8va)
End Fill 1
Bass Fig. 1
Harm.

D5 C5
thoughts ar - rive like but - ter - flies. Oh,
D5 Bb5 D5 C5
he don't know, so he chas - es them a-way.
D5 Bb5
Oh, some-day yet he'll be - gin his
D.S. al Coda 1
D5 C5 D5 C5 D5 C5
life a - gain, life a - gain, life a - gain.
End Bass Fig. 1
Coda 1
Chorus
w/ Bass Fill 1
w/ Bass Fig. 1
D5 Bb5 D5 C5
Ev - en flow, thoughts ar - rive like but - ter - flies.

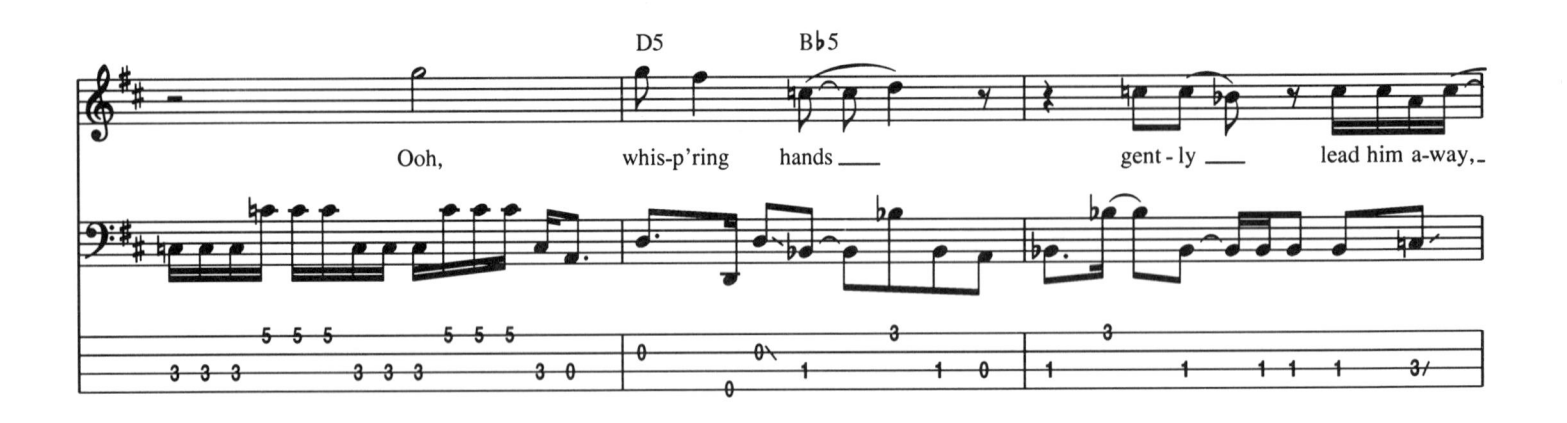

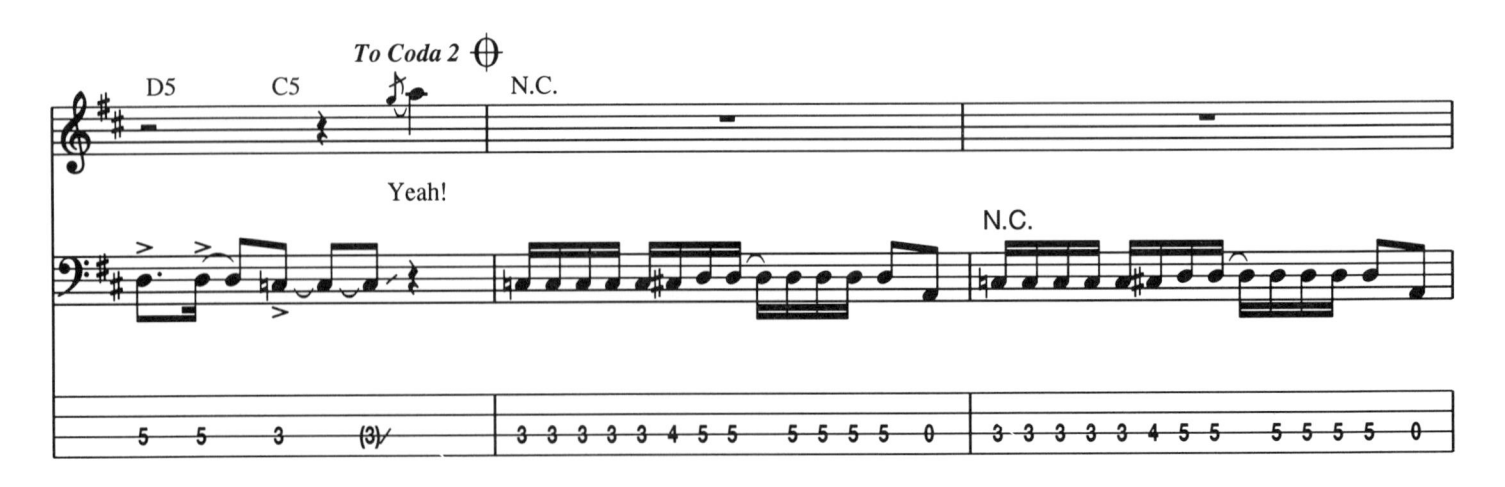

Oh, he don't know, so he chas-es them a-way.

Oh, some-day yet he'll be-gin his life a-gain.

Ooh, whis-p'ring hands gent-ly lead him a-way,

him a-way, him a-way.

To Coda 2

Yeah!

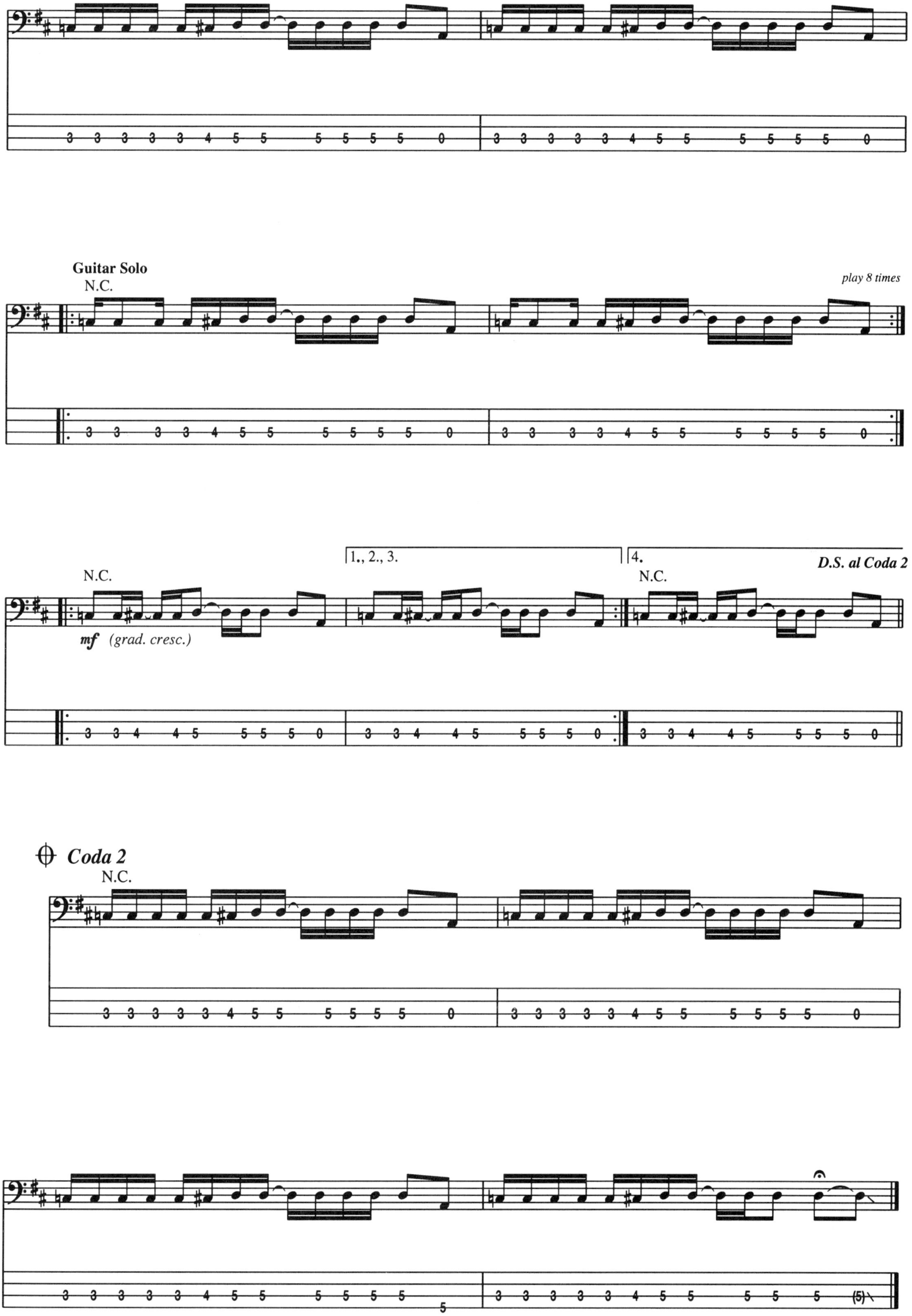
Guitar Solo
N.C.
play 8 times
1., 2., 3.
4.
N.C.
D.S. al Coda 2
N.C.
mf (grad. cresc.)
Coda 2
N.C.

Alive

Music by Stone Gossard
Lyric by Eddie Vedder

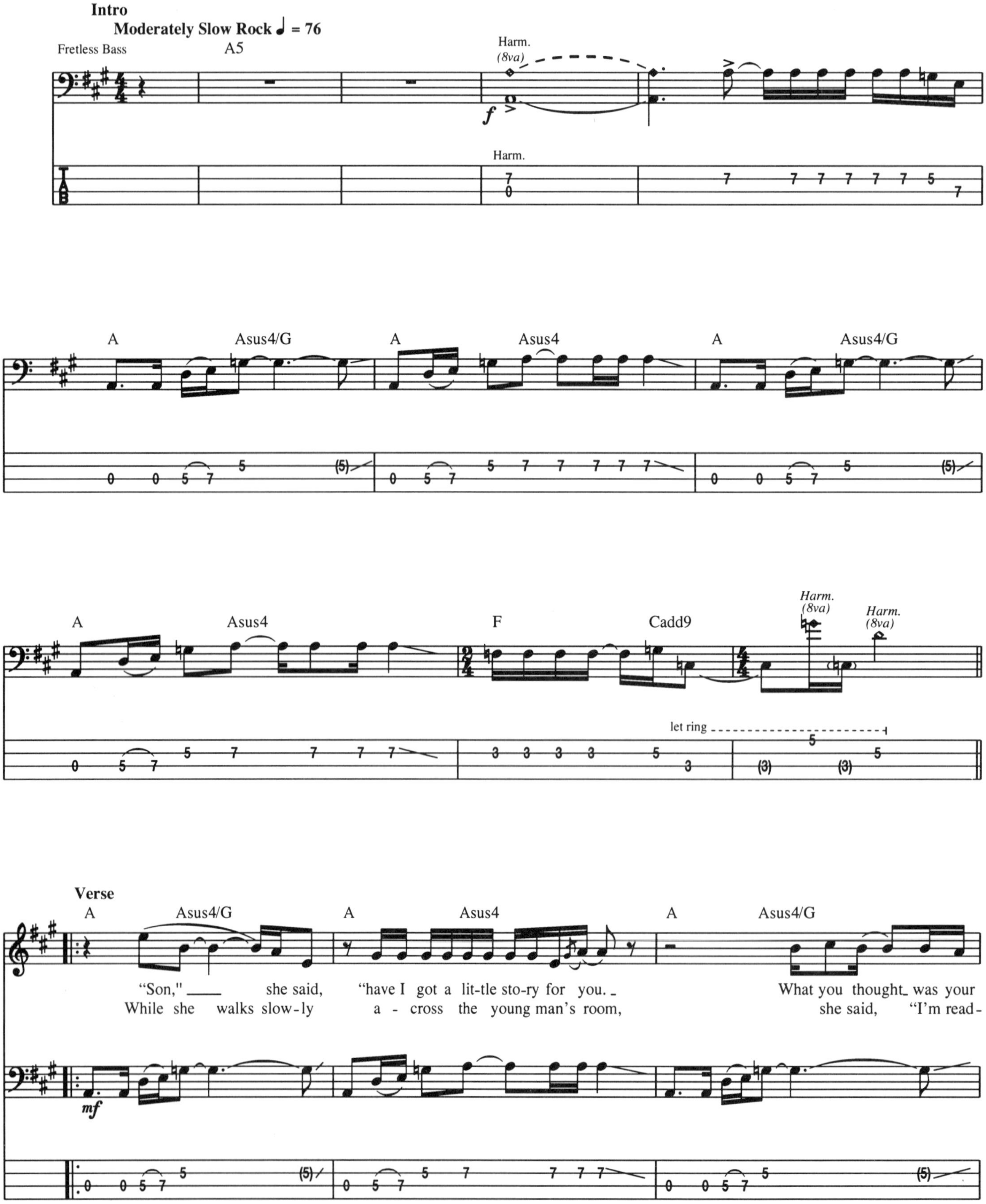

A Asus4 A Asus4/G A Asus4
dad-dy was nothin' ___ but a... While _ you were sit - ting home a - lone _ at age _ thir - teen,
y for you." I ___ can't re-mem-ber an - y - thing _ to this ver - y day,
A Asus4/G A Asus4 F Cadd9
your real dad - dy was dy - ing. Sor-ry you did-n't see him, _ but I'm ___ glad _
'cept the look, the look. ___ Oh, you know where. _ Now
Harm. (8va) Harm. (8va)
let ring
Harm. Harm.
Chorus
F C E G D A
___ we talked." _ Oh, ___ I, ___ oh, ___ I'm still a - live. _ Hey ___
I can't see, ___ I just stare. ___ I, ___
f
1.
E G D A E G
I, ___ oh, ___ I'm still a - live. _ Hey ___ I, ___ oh, ___

16

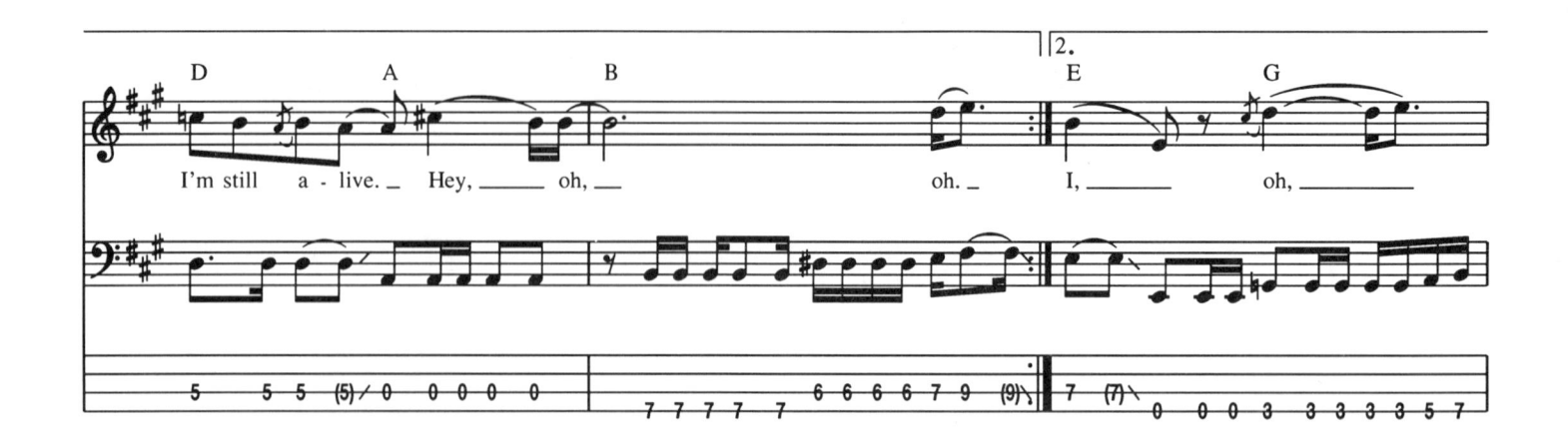

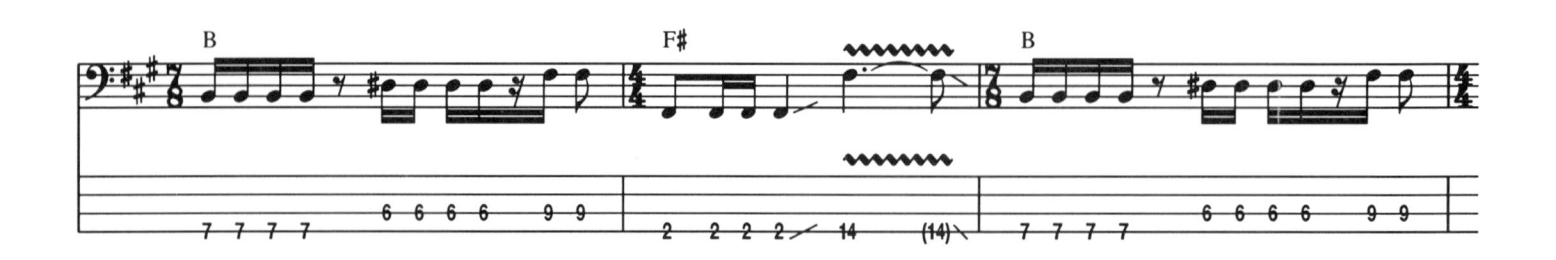

Bridge
A7/C♯ A9/B Dsus2
A7/C♯ A9/E D5(add6)
A7/C♯ A9/B Dsus2
"Is some-thing wrong?" she said. Of course there is. "You're still a-
Harm.
8va
15ma
mf
A7/C♯ A9/E D5(add6)
B7sus4/D♯ B9/C♯ Esus2
B7/D♯ B7/F♯ E6sus2
live," she said. Oh, n' do I de-serve to be? Is that the ques-tion? And if so,
D.S. al Coda
(take 2nd ending)
B7/D♯ B9/C♯ Esus2
B7/D♯ B9/C♯ E6sus2
if so, who an - swers? Who an - swers?
Coda
Guitar Solo
E G D A E G
D A E G D A

E G D A E G
D A E G D A
Double Time Feel
play 4 times
E G D A E G
D A E G D A
E G D A E G
D A E G
play 4 times
D A E
Free Time
full
full
full
rit.

Why Go

Music by Jeff Ament
Lyric by Eddie Vedder

years and counting since they put her in this
er, but what they want her to be is

place. She's been di-ag-nosed by some stu-pid fuck, and
weak. She could play pre-tend, she could join the game, boy.

Mom-my a-grees, yeah.
She could be an-oth-er clone.

Why go home? Why go home? Why go home?

Ooh.

Chorus
Em Bm G D Em Bm
Why go home? Why go home? Why go home?
To Coda
G D Em Bm G D
Why go home? What you taught me put me here. Don't come
(Why go home?) (Why go home?)
Em Cmaj7 N.C. (E5) (D5)
vis-it, Mother. Sing it.
(Why go home?)
Guitar Solo
(Em7)

D.S. al Coda
Coda
Em Bm G D Em Bm
vis-it, mother-er, moth-er, yeah. Why go home?
(Why go home?) (Why go home?)
G D Em Bm G D
Why go home? Why go home? Why go home?
Em Bm G D Em Cmaj7
Why go home? Why go home? Why go home?
Free Time
N.C.(E5) (D5) E7#9
Why?

Black

Music by Stone Gossard
Lyric by Eddie Vedder

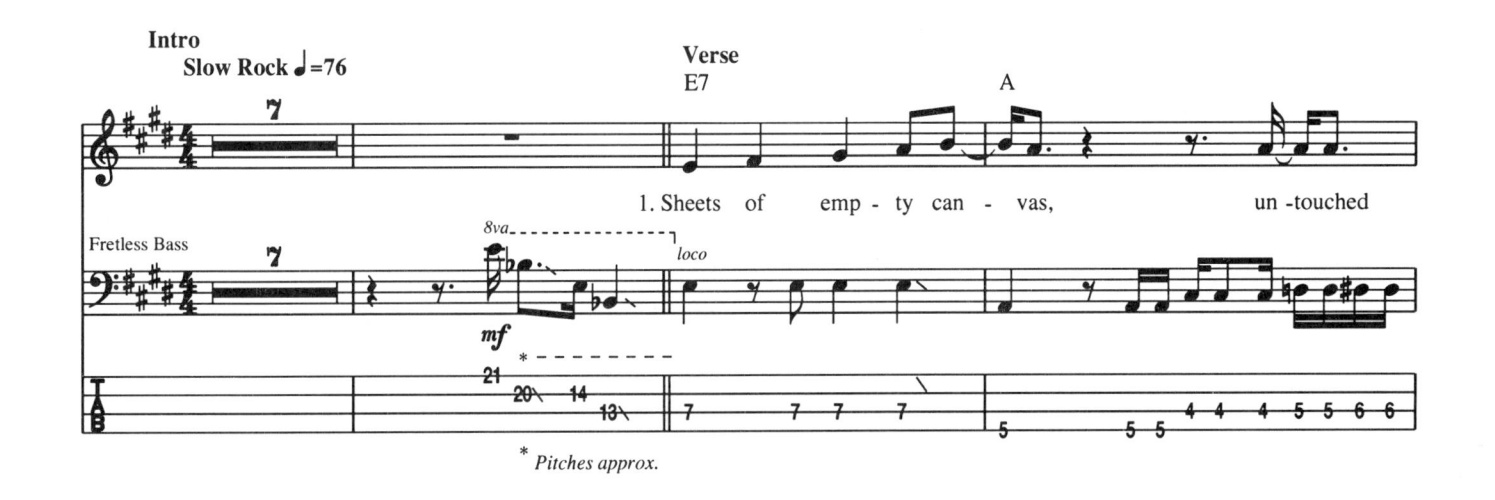

Intro — Slow Rock ♩=76
Verse

1. Sheets of empty canvas, untouched sheets of clay. Her lace spread out before me as her body once did. Ooh, all five horizons revolved around her sun, as the earth to the sun. Now the air I tasted and breathed, has

2. I take a walk outside; I'm surrounded by some kids at play. I can feel their laughter, so

Copyright © 1991 PolyGram International Publishing, Inc., Write Treatage Music, Scribing C-Ment Songs and Innocent Bystander
International Copyright Secured   All Rights Reserved

Pre-chorus
E
C5
tak-en a turn. Ooh, and all I taught her was ev-'ry-thing.
why do I sear ? Ooh, and twist-ed thoughts that spin 'round my
let ring
w/Bass Fill 1, 2nd time
E5
G5
C5
Ooh, I know she gave me all that she
head. I'm spin-ning, oh, I'm spin-ning. How quick the sun can drop a-way.
Chorus
E5
D5
C5
E5
wore. And now my bit-ter hands shake be-neath the clouds of what was ev-'ry-thing.
And now my bit-ter hands cra-dle brok-en glass of what was ev-'ry-thing.
D5
C5
1.
E5
Oh, the pic-ture's sad, all been washed in black, tat-tooed ev-'ry-thing.
Oh, the pic-ture's sad, all been washed in
Bass Fill 1

2.
E5 D5 C5 D5
black, tat-tooed ev-'ry-thing. All the love gone bad turned my world to black, tat-tooed all I
C5 E5 D5 C5
see, all that I am, all I'll be. Yeah.
E5 D5 C5 E5
Uh huh, uh huh. I
D5 C5 E5
know some day you'll have a beau-ti-ful life, I know you'll be a star in some-bod-y els-e's sky. But why,
D5 C5 E5
why, why, can't it be, uh, can't it be mine?

D5
C5
E5
with vocal ad lib till end
C5
1., 2., 3., 4.
E5
5.
D5
C5
E5
D5
C5
E5
D5
C5
E5
Repeat and Fade
D5
C5
E5

Jeremy

Music by Jeff Ament
Lyric by Eddie Vedder

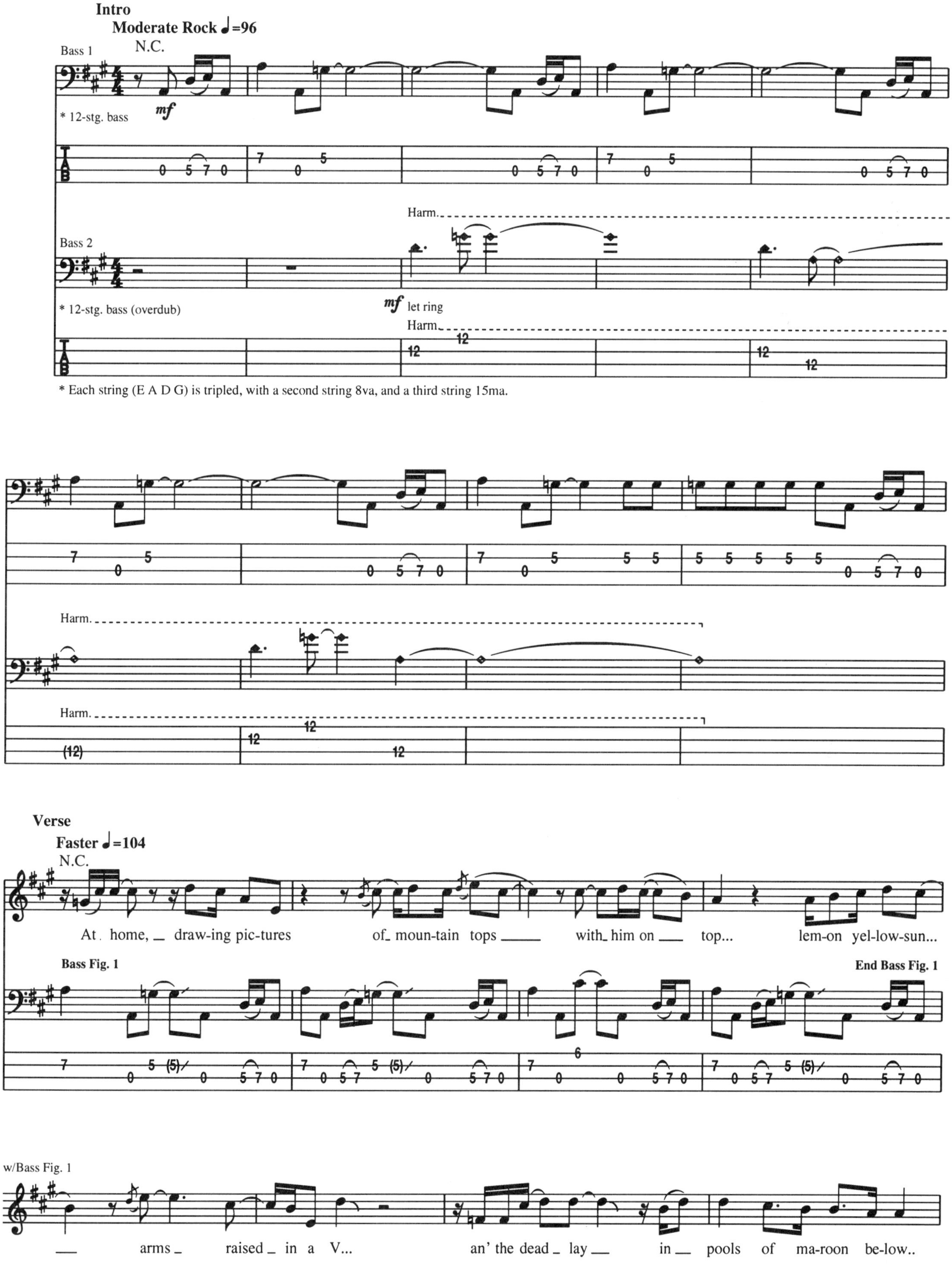

*A5 G5 D/F♯ A7sus4 A5
Dad-dy did-n't give at-ten-tion... oh, to the fact that Mom-my did-n't
Bass Fig. 2
f
* Chords refer to guitar.
G5 D/F♯ A7sus4 A5
care... King Jer-e-my the wick-ed... oh, ruled his world.
End Bass Fig. 2
Chorus
A7sus2 Fsus2 D5 E5 F5 A5
Jer-e-my spoke in class to-day.
A7sus2 Fsus2 D5 E5 F5/C A5
Jer-e-my spoke in class to-day.
w/Bass Fig. 1, 4 times
Verse
N.C.
Clear-ly I re-mem-ber... pick-ing on the boy... seemed a harm-less
lit-tle fuck... oo, but we un-leashed a li-on... gnashed
his teeth an' bit the re-cess lad-y's breast... how could I for-
get... an' he hit me with a sur-prise left... my jaw left hurt-in'...

oo, dropped wide o-pen... just like the day... oh,
w/Bass Fig. 2
A5 G5
like the day I heard... Dad-dy did-n't
D/F# A7sus4 A5
give af-fec-tion, no... and the boy was some-thing that Mom-my would-n't
G5 D/F# A7sus4 A5
wear... King Jer-e-my the wick-ed... oh, ruled his world.
Chorus
A7sus2 F(sus2) D5 E5 F5 A5
Jer-e-my spoke in class to-day.
(...day.)
A5 G5 Dm E5 F5/C A5
Jer-e-my spoke in class to-day.
(...day.)
A7sus2 Fsus2 D5 E5 F5 A5
Jer-e-my spoke in class to-day!
(steady gliss.)
Interlude
N.C.
Oo, oo, oo, oo, oo, oo, oo, oo, oo, oo, oo, oo, oo, oo. Try to for-get

this...   Try   to e-rase   this...
(Try   to forget this...)   (Try   to e-rase

Chorus
Asus2   N.C.(F)   D5   E5   F5   A5   N.C.

from the black - board.
this...)

Am/C   Asus2 Gsus4   D5   E5   N.C.   A5

Jer - e-my spoke in   class   to - day.

A7sus2 Fsus2   D5   E5   F5   A5

Jer - e-my spoke in   class   to - day.
(day...)

Asus2 Gsus4   D5   E5   N.C.   A5

Jer - e-my spoke in,   spoke in,   Jer - e-my spoke in,   spoke in,

*Chords refer to bass.

Jer-e-my spoke in class to-day.

Oceans

Music by Stone Gossard and Jeff Ament
Lyric by Eddie Vedder

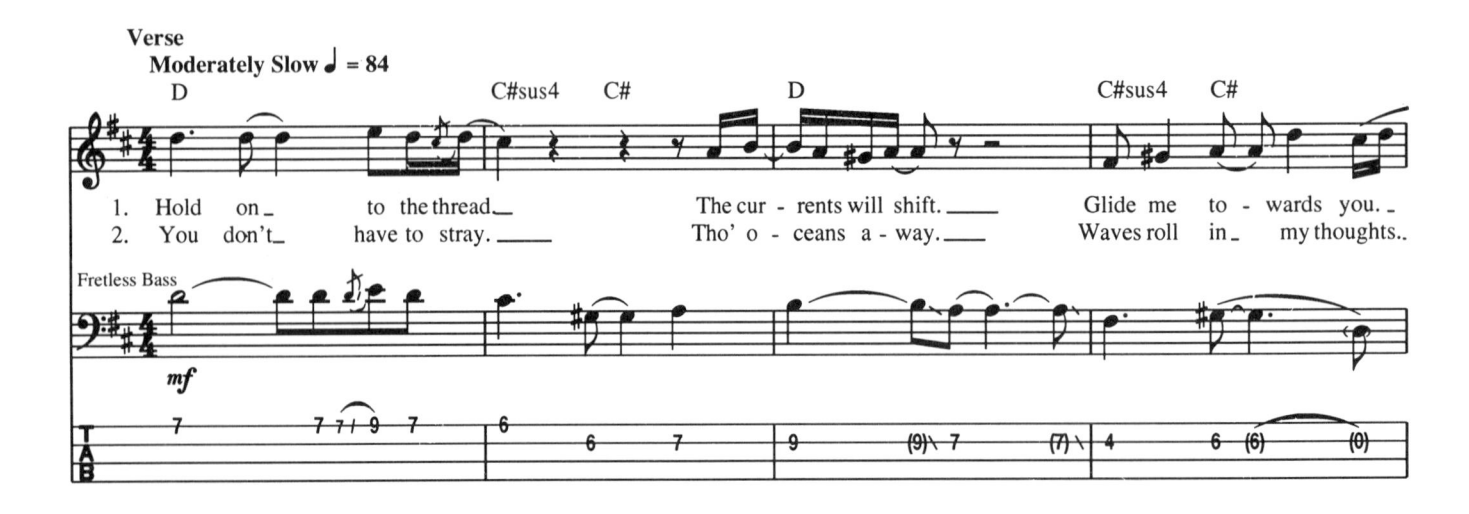

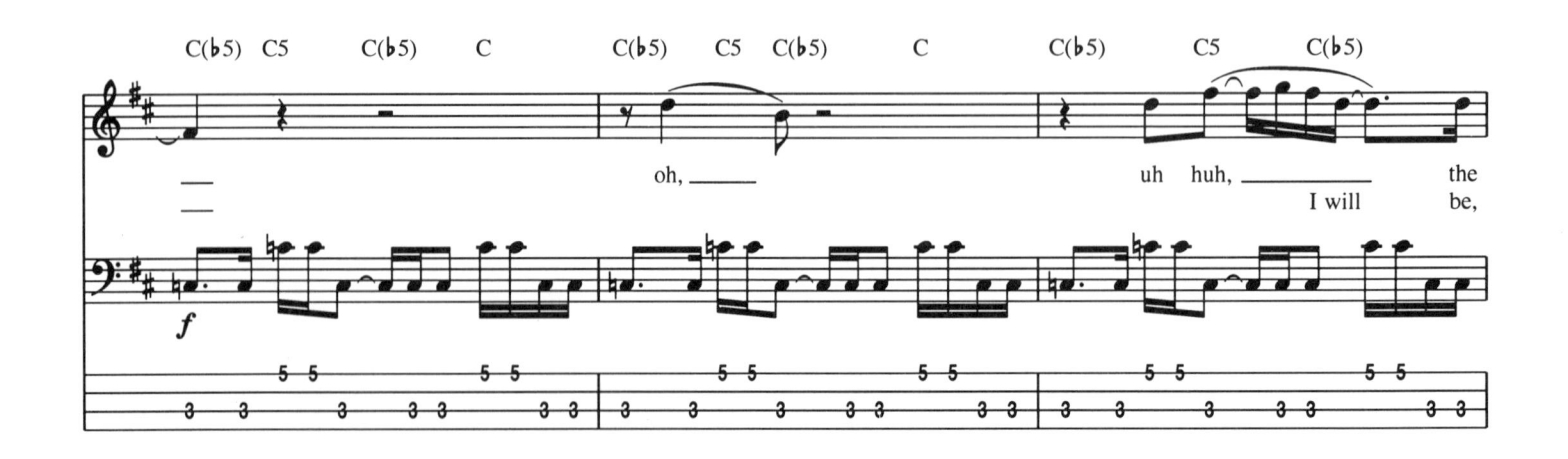

Verse
Moderately Slow ♩ = 84

1. Hold on to the thread. The currents will shift. Glide me towards you.
2. You don't have to stray. Tho' oceans away. Waves roll in my thoughts.

Know something's left. And we're all allowed to dream of the next,
Hold tight the ring. The sea will rise. Please stand by the shore

oh, uh huh, the
I will be,

Copyright © 1991 PolyGram International Publishing, Inc., Write Treatage Music, Scribing C-Ment Songs and Innocent Bystander
International Copyright Secured   All Rights Reserved

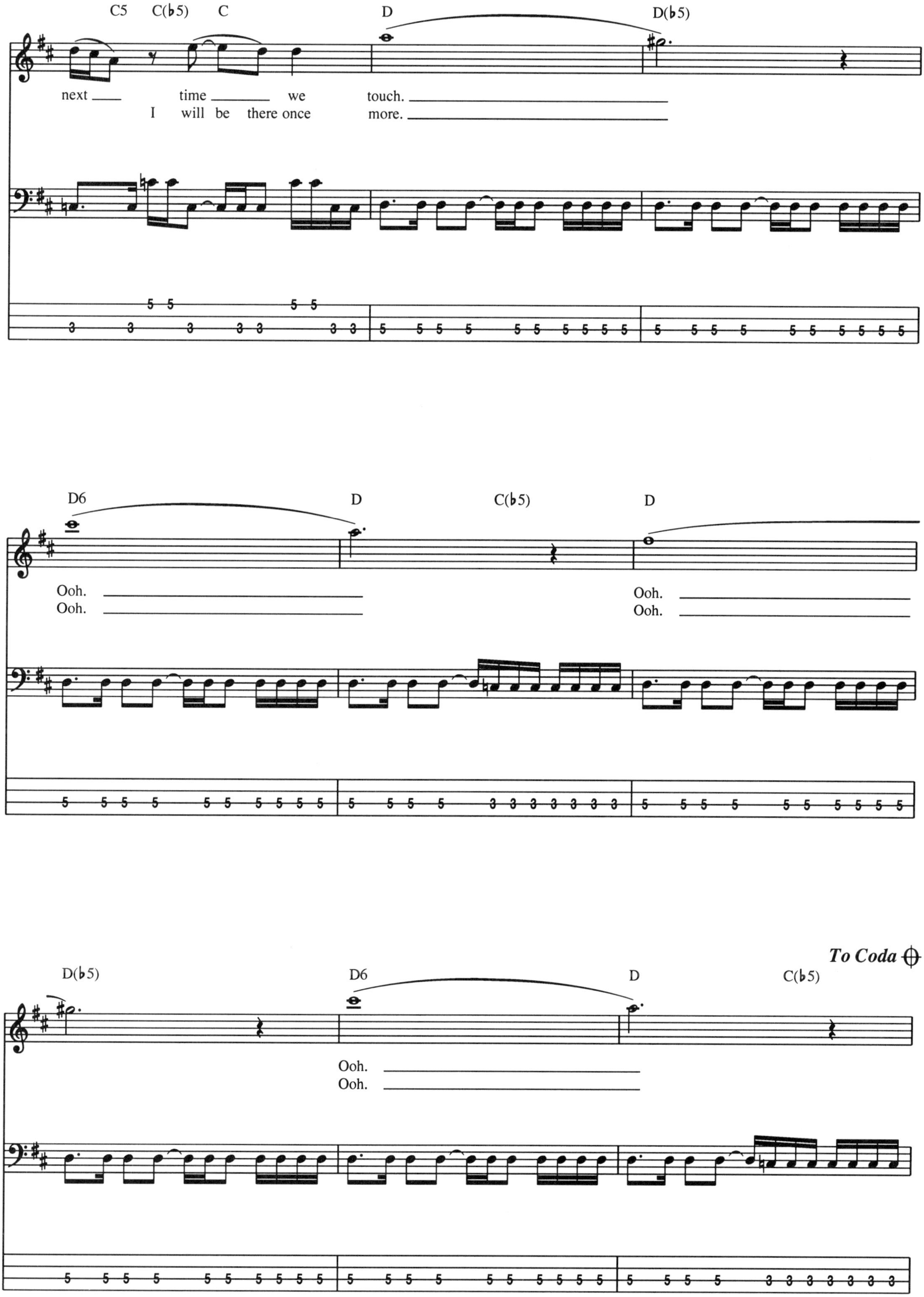
C5 C(♭5) C
D
D(♭5)
next ___ time ___ we touch. ___
I will be there once more. ___
D6
D
C(♭5)
D
Ooh. ___
Ooh. ___
Ooh. ___
Ooh. ___
To Coda
D(♭5)
D6
D
C(♭5)
Ooh. ___
Ooh. ___

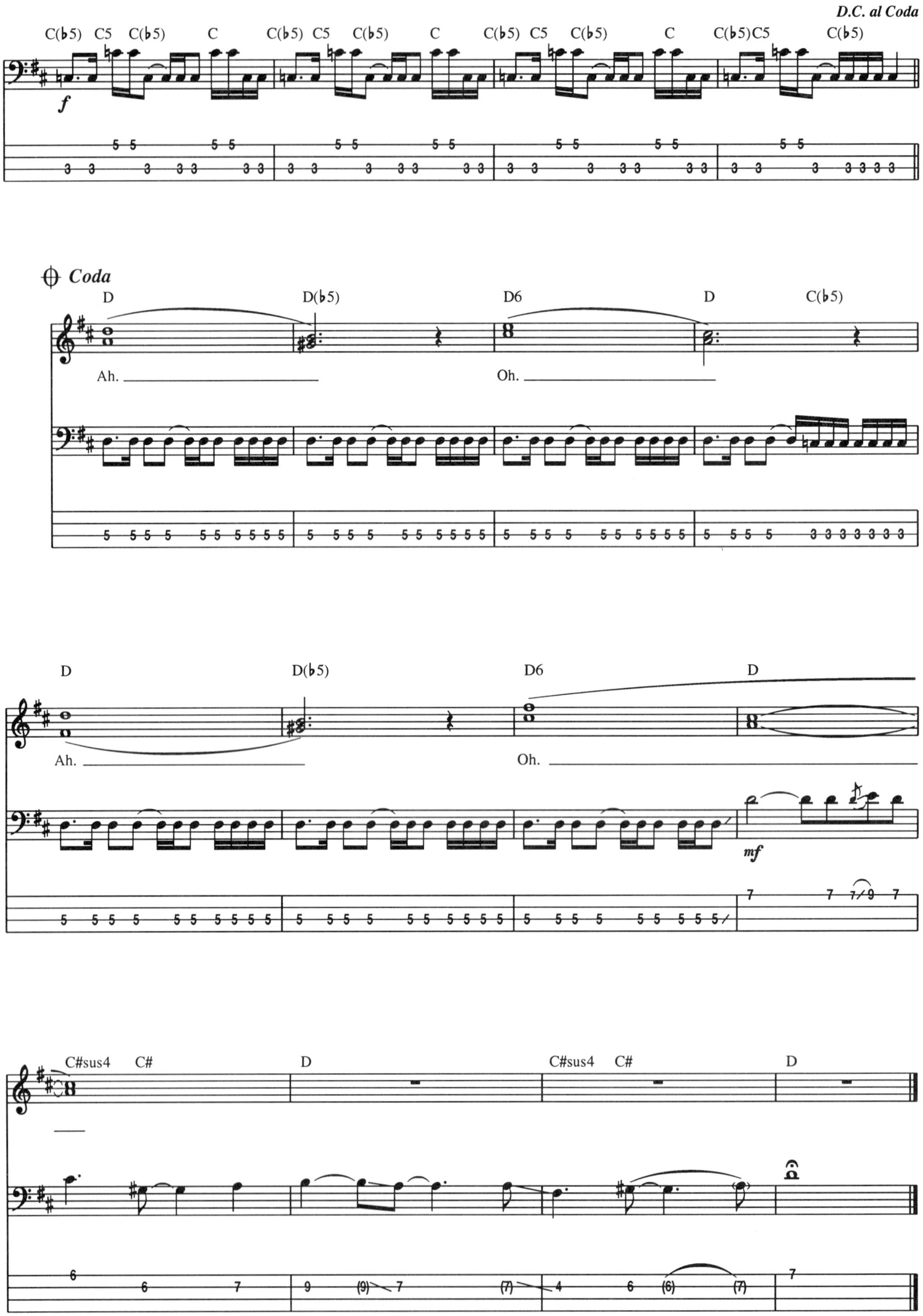
D.C. al Coda
C(♭5) C5 C(♭5) C C(♭5) C5 C(♭5) C C(♭5) C5 C(♭5) C C(♭5)C5 C(♭5)
f
Coda
D D(♭5) D6 D C(♭5)
Ah.
Oh.
D D(♭5) D6 D
Ah.
Oh.
mf
C#sus4 C# D C#sus4 C# D

Porch

Words and Music by Eddie Vedder

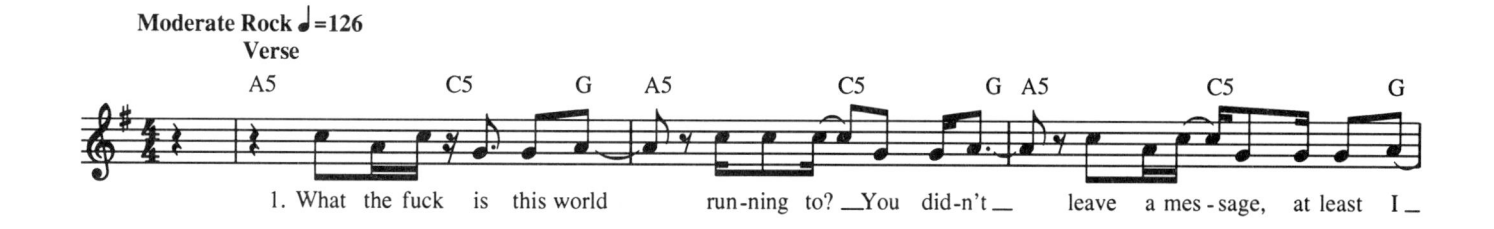

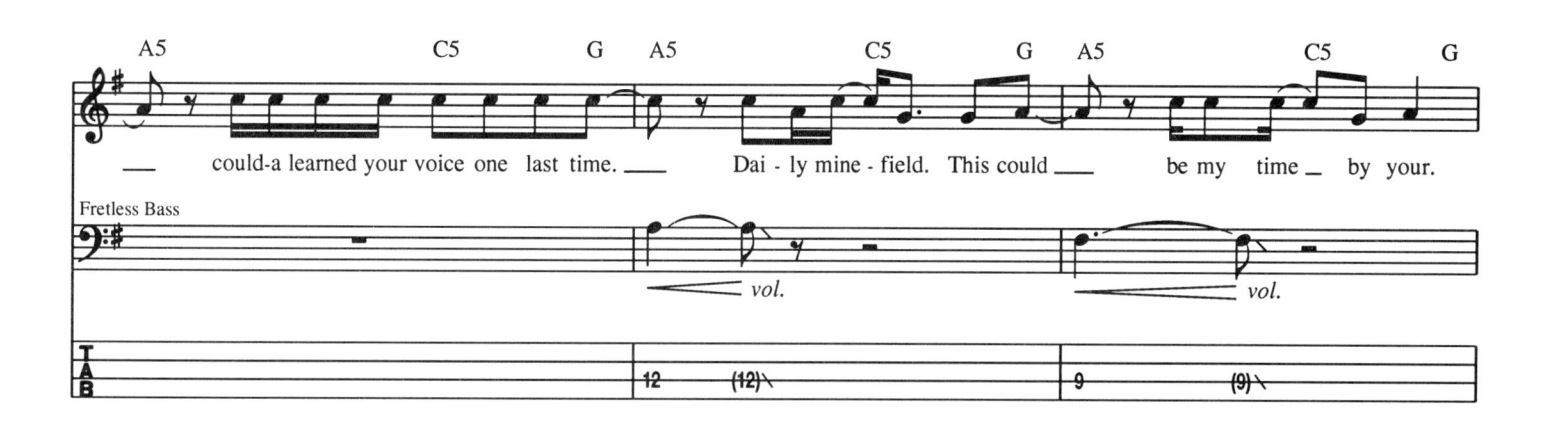

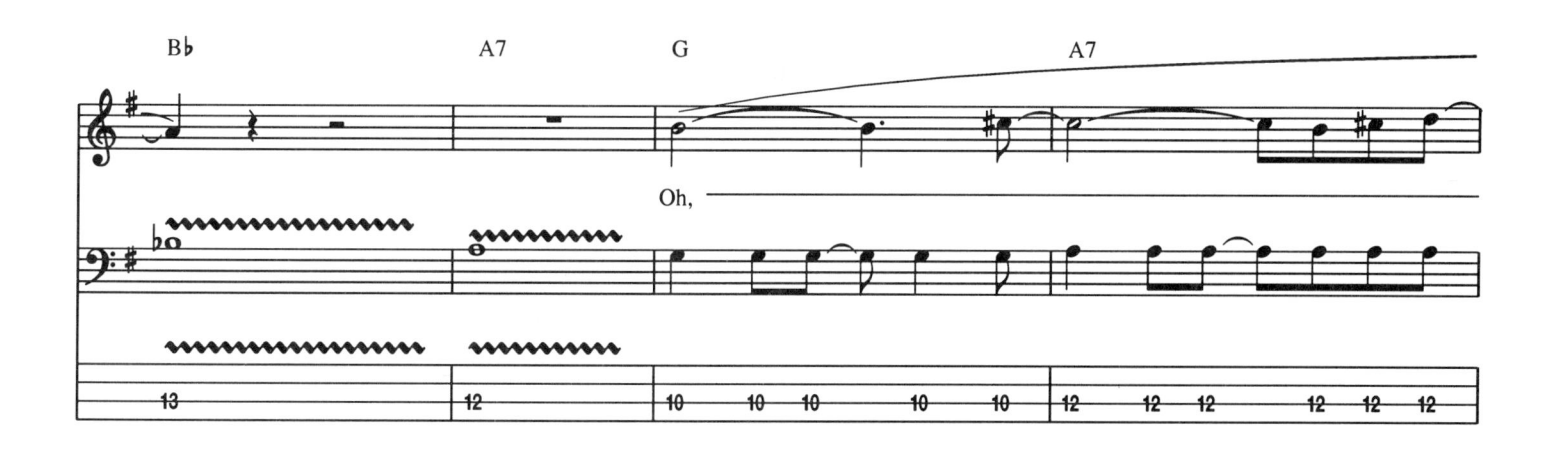

Moderate Rock ♩=126
Verse

1. What the fuck is this world running to? You didn't leave a message, at least I could-a learned your voice one last time. Daily mine-field. This could be my time by your. Would you hit me? Would you hit me? Oh. Oh,

Copyright © 1991 Innocent Bystander
International Copyright Secured All Rights Reserved

Bb C A5 C5 G
wow!
A5 C5 G A5 C5 G A5 C5 G
Verse
A5 C5 G A5 C5 G A5 C5 G
2. All the bills go by and in-i-tia-tives are tak-en up by the mid-dle.
A5 C5 G A5 C5 G A5 C5 G
There ain't gon-na be an-y mid-dle an-y-more. And the cross. I'm bear-in' home ain't in-dic-a-tive of my
A5 C5 G A5
Chorus
G A
place. Left the porch. Left the porch. Oh.

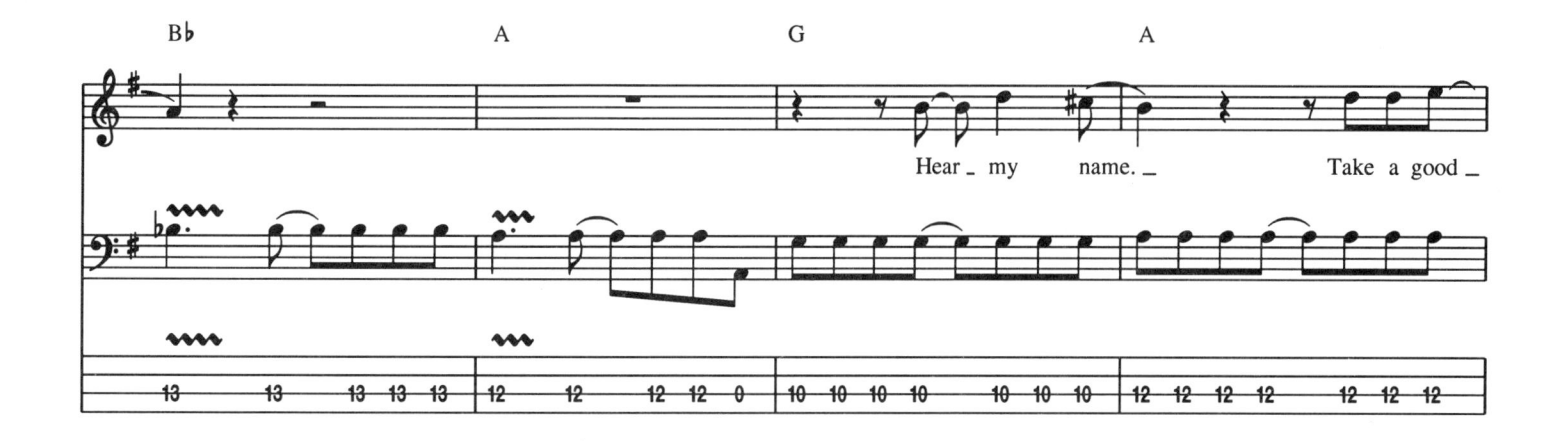

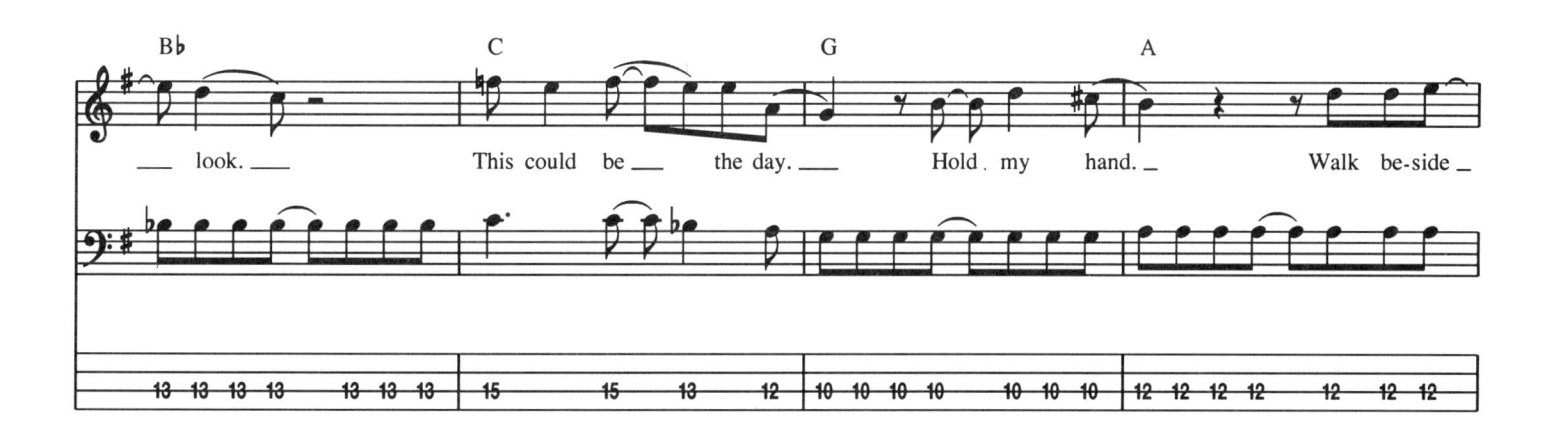

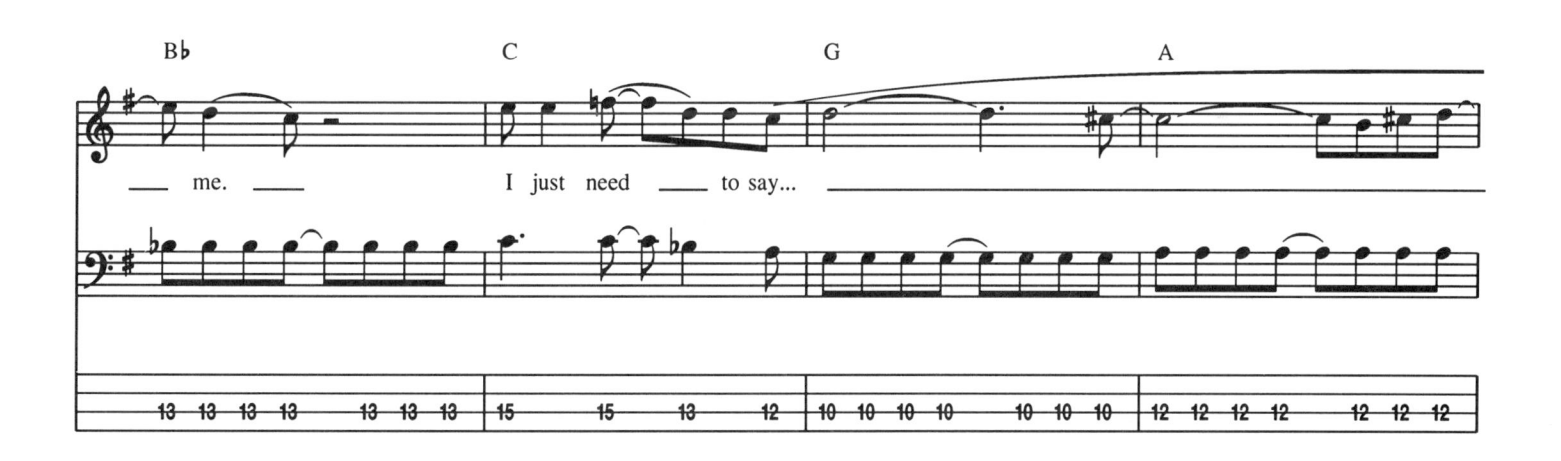

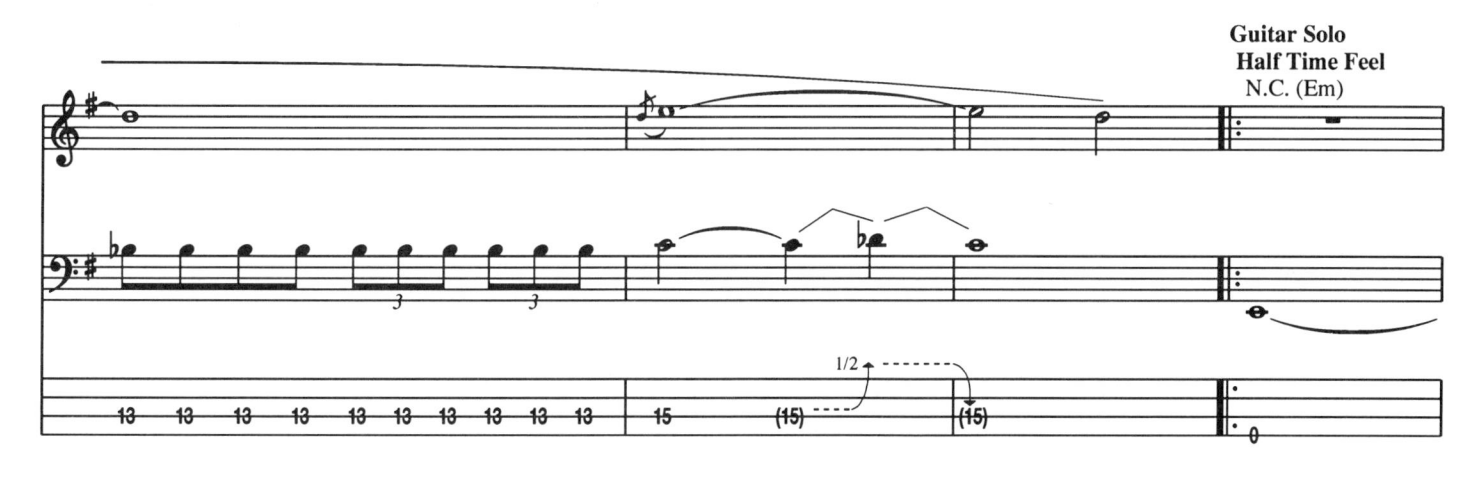

Lyrics:
Hear my name. Take a good look. This could be the day. Hold my hand. Walk beside me. I just need to say...

Guitar Solo
Half Time Feel
N.C. (Em)

Play 6 times
A
Harm.
let ring
Harm.
mf
cresc.
G
A7
B♭
C
Hear my name. Take a good look. This could be the day.
f
Hold my hand. Lie be-side me. I just need to say.

G
A7
B♭
C
I could not take a - just one day
I know when I would not ev - er touch
G
A7
B♭
C
you, hold you, feel you, ev - er
nev - er a - gain
G
A7
B♭
Yeah.
Yeah.
Yeah.
1., 2., 3.
4.
C
C
N.C.(Em)
mp
let ring

Garden

Music by Stone Gossard and Jeff Ament
Lyric by Eddie Vedder

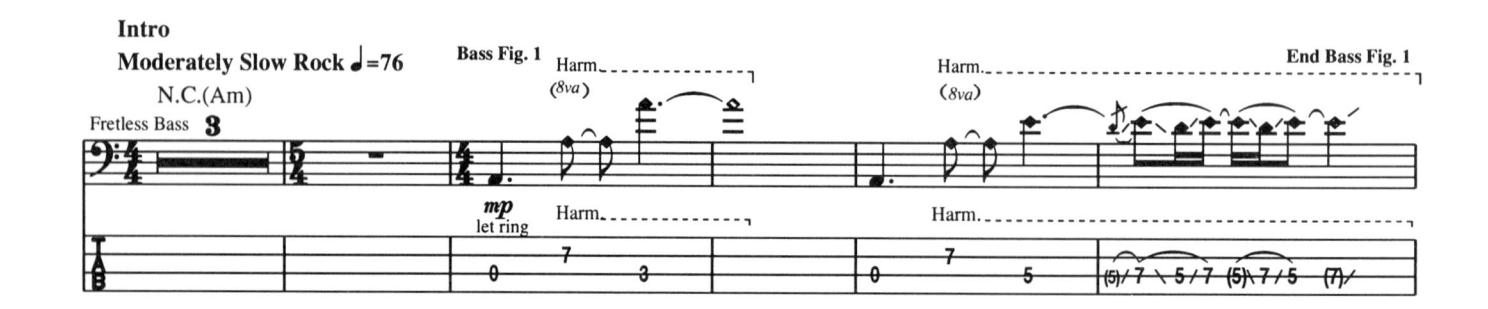

Chorus
Am G G/D Am
walk with my hands bound. I will walk with my
(Walk.) (Walk.)
Bass Fig. 2
f
let ring
G G/D Am G G/D Am
face blood. I will walk with my shad-ow flag in - to your gar - den,
(Walk.)
End Bass Fig. 2
let ring
G G/D N.C. (Am)
gar - den of stone.
mf
let ring
Verse
N.C. (Am)
2. Af - ter all is done and we're still a-lone, I won't be tak-en, yet I'll
let ring
w/Bass Fig. 2
Chorus
Am G G/D Am G G/D
go with my hands bound. I will walk with my face blood. I will
(Go.) (Walk.)

Am G G/D Am
walk ___ with my shad-ow ___ flag ___ in - to your gar - den, ___
(Walk)
Bridge
G G/D A5 G5 F#5 D5 A5 G5 F#5 D5 A5 G5 F#5 D5
___ gar - den ___ of stone, ___ yeah.
(Oh.) ___
A5 G5 F#5 D5 A5 G5 F#5 D5 A5 G5 F#5 D5
I ___ don't show. ___ I ___ don't ___ share. ___ I ___ don't ___
A5 G5 F#5 D5 A5 G5 F#5 D5
need, ___ yeah, ___ what you have to give, ___ yeah.
Harm.
8va
let ring
Harm.
Guitar Solo
Am

Harm.
8va
Harm.
Harm.
8va
Harm.
Chorus
Am
G
G/D
Am
Ooh, I will walk with my hands bound. I will walk with my
(Walk.)
(Walk.)
G
G/D
Am
G
G/D
face blood. I will walk with my shad-ow flag in -
(Walk.)

44

Deep

Music by Stone Gossard and Jeff Ament
Lyric by Eddie Vedder

deep, 'eah. Uh. Can't touch the bot-tom. Oh, In too

Bridge

deep.

Guitar Solo

Oh.

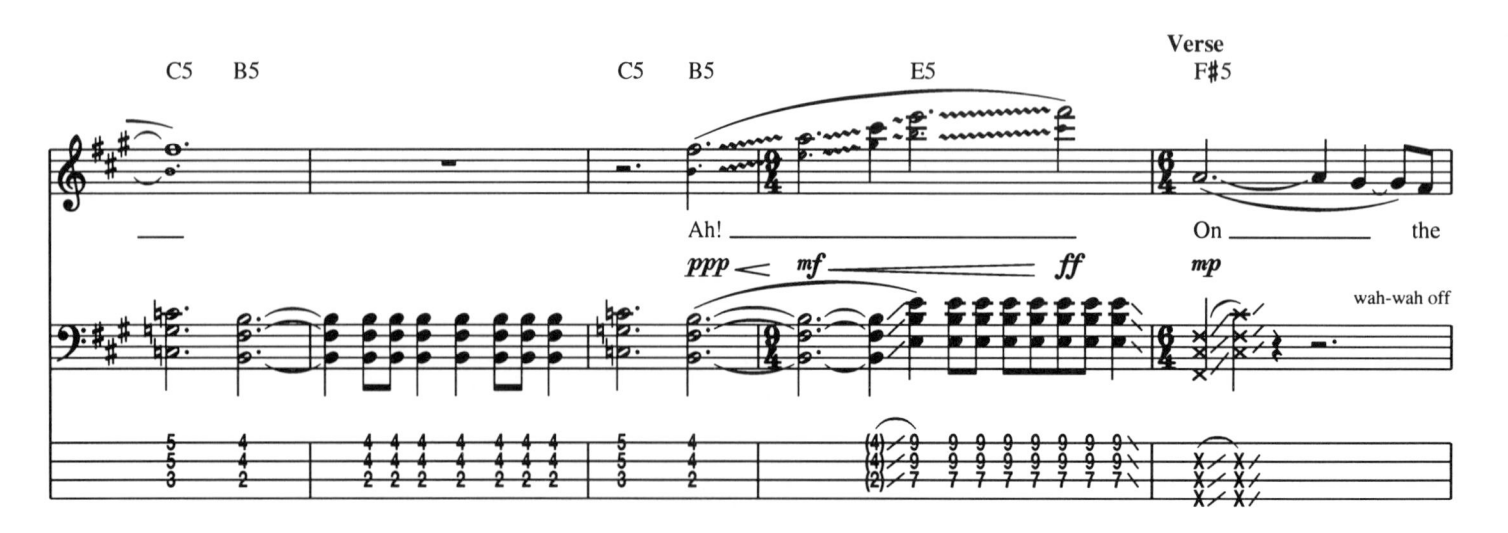

Ah! On the

edge of a Christ-mas clean love. Young vir-gin from heav-en, vis-it-ing hell. To the man a-bove her, she just ain't noth-in'. And she doesn't like the view. She doesn't like the view. She doesn't like the view, but he sinks him-self

D.S. al Coda
(take 2nd ending)

Coda

Oh, oh, oh, 'eah, the bot-tom. Hey.

Free time

Oh, oh, oh.

Bass Fill 1
Bass Gtr. 1

Release

Music by Stone Gossard, Jeff Ament, Mike McCready and Dave Krusen
Lyric by Eddie Vedder

D Bm11 C D Bm11 C
D Bm11 C D Bm11 C
D Bm11 C D Bm11 C
D Bm11 C D Bm11 C
Verse
D Bm11 C D Bm11 C
D Bm11 C D Bm11 C
Harm.
(8va)
let ring
Harm.

D Bm11 C D Bm11 C
Harm. (8va)
let ring Harm.
D Bm11 C D Bm11 C
D Bm11 C D Bm11 C
f
D Bm11 C D Bm11 C
Verse
D Bm11 C D Bm11 C
mf
let ring Harm.

D
Bm11
C
D
Bm11
C
Harm.
(8va)
let ring
Harm.
D
Bm11
C
D
Bm11
C
Harm.
(8va)
let ring
Harm.
D
Bm11
C
D
Bm11
C
D
Bm11
C
D
Bm11
Bm11
C
D
Bm11
C
D
Bm11
C

D
Bm11
C
Freely
Bm7
Harm.
(8va)
let ring
mp
p
Tag ♩ =80
D7
Repeat and Fade
fade in

RECORDED VERSIONS
The Best Note-For-Note Transcriptions Available

ALL BOOKS INCLUDE TABLATURE

Number	Title	Price
00690016	Will Ackerman Collection	$19.95
00690146	Aerosmith – Toys in the Attic	$19.95
00694865	Alice In Chains – Dirt	$19.95
00694932	Allman Brothers Band – Volume 1	$24.95
00694933	Allman Brothers Band – Volume 2	$24.95
00694934	Allman Brothers Band – Volume 3	$24.95
00694877	Chet Atkins – Guitars For All Seasons	$19.95
00690418	Best of Audio Adrenaline	$17.95
00694918	Randy Bachman Collection	$22.95
00690366	Bad Company Original Anthology - Bk 1	$19.95
00690367	Bad Company Original Anthology - Bk 2	$19.95
00694880	Beatles – Abbey Road	$19.95
00694863	Beatles – Sgt. Pepper's Lonely Hearts Club Band	$19.95
00690383	Beatles – Yellow Submarine	$19.95
00690174	Beck – Mellow Gold	$17.95
00690346	Beck – Mutations	$19.95
00690175	Beck – Odelay	$17.95
00694884	The Best of George Benson	$19.95
00692385	Chuck Berry	$19.95
00692200	Black Sabbath – We Sold Our Soul For Rock 'N' Roll	$19.95
00690115	Blind Melon – Soup	$19.95
00690305	Blink 182 – Dude Ranch	$19.95
00690028	Blue Oyster Cult – Cult Classics	$19.95
00690219	Blur	$19.95
00690168	Roy Buchanon Collection	$19.95
00690364	Cake – Songbook	$19.95
00690337	Jerry Cantrell – Boggy Depot	$19.95
00690293	Best of Steven Curtis Chapman	$19.95
00690043	Cheap Trick – Best Of	$19.95
00690171	Chicago – Definitive Guitar Collection	$22.95
00690415	Clapton Chronicles – Best of Eric Clapton	$17.95
00690393	Eric Clapton – Selections from Blues	$19.95
00660139	Eric Clapton – Journeyman	$19.95
00694869	Eric Clapton – Live Acoustic	$19.95
00694896	John Mayall/Eric Clapton – Bluesbreakers	$19.95
00690162	Best of the Clash	$19.95
00690166	Albert Collins – The Alligator Years	$16.95
00694940	Counting Crows – August & Everything After	$19.95
00690197	Counting Crows – Recovering the Satellites	$19.95
00694840	Cream – Disraeli Gears	$19.95
00690401	Creed – Human Clay	$19.95
00690352	Creed – My Own Prison	$19.95
00690184	dc Talk – Jesus Freak	$19.95
00690333	dc Talk – Supernatural	$19.95
00660186	Alex De Grassi Guitar Collection	$19.95
00690289	Best of Deep Purple	$17.95
00694831	Derek And The Dominos – Layla & Other Assorted Love Songs	$19.95
00690322	Ani Di Franco – Little Plastic Castle	$19.95
00690187	Dire Straits – Brothers In Arms	$19.95
00690191	Dire Straits – Money For Nothing	$24.95
00695382	The Very Best of Dire Straits – Sultans of Swing	$19.95
00660178	Willie Dixon – Master Blues Composer	$24.95
00690250	Best of Duane Eddy	$16.95
00690349	Eve 6	$19.95
00313164	Eve 6 – Horrorscope	$19.95
00690323	Fastball – All the Pain Money Can Buy	$19.95
00690089	Foo Fighters	$19.95
00690235	Foo Fighters – The Colour and the Shape	$19.95
00690394	Foo Fighters – There Is Nothing Left to Lose	$19.95
00690222	G3 Live – Satriani, Vai, Johnson	$22.95
00694807	Danny Gatton – 88 Elmira St	$19.95
00690438	Genesis Guitar Anthology	$19.95
00690127	Goo Goo Dolls – A Boy Named Goo	$19.95
00690338	Goo Goo Dolls – Dizzy Up the Girl	$19.95
00690117	John Gorka Collection	$19.95
00690114	Buddy Guy Collection Vol. A-J	$22.95
00690193	Buddy Guy Collection Vol. L-Y	$22.95
00694798	George Harrison Anthology	$19.95
00690068	Return Of The Hellecasters	$19.95
00692930	Jimi Hendrix – Are You Experienced?	$24.95
00692931	Jimi Hendrix – Axis: Bold As Love	$22.95
00692932	Jimi Hendrix – Electric Ladyland	$24.95
00690218	Jimi Hendrix – First Rays of the New Rising Sun	$27.95
00690038	Gary Hoey – Best Of	$19.95
00660029	Buddy Holly	$19.95
00660169	John Lee Hooker – A Blues Legend	$19.95
00690054	Hootie & The Blowfish – Cracked Rear View	$19.95
00694905	Howlin' Wolf	$19.95
00690136	Indigo Girls – 1200 Curfews	$22.95
00694938	Elmore James – Master Electric Slide Guitar	$19.95
00690167	Skip James Blues Guitar Collection	$16.95
00694833	Billy Joel For Guitar	$19.95
00694912	Eric Johnson – Ah Via Musicom	$19.95
00690169	Eric Johnson – Venus Isle	$22.95
00694799	Robert Johnson – At The Crossroads	$19.95
00693185	Judas Priest – Vintage Hits	$19.95
00690277	Best of Kansas	$19.95
00690073	B. B. King – 1950-1957	$24.95
00690098	B. B. King – 1958-1967	$24.95
00690444	B.B. King and Eric Clapton – Riding with the King	$19.95
00690134	Freddie King Collection	$17.95
00690157	Kiss – Alive	$19.95
00690163	Mark Knopfler/Chet Atkins – Neck and Neck	$19.95
00690296	Patty Larkin Songbook	$17.95
00690018	Living Colour – Best Of	$19.95
00694845	Yngwie Malmsteen – Fire And Ice	$19.95
00694956	Bob Marley – Legend	$19.95
00690283	Best of Sarah McLachlan	$19.95
00690382	Sarah McLachlan – Mirrorball	$19.95
00690354	Sarah McLachlan – Surfacing	$19.95
00690442	Matchbox 20 – Mad Season	$19.95
00690239	Matchbox 20 – Yourself or Someone Like You	$19.95
00690244	Megadeath – Cryptic Writings	$19.95
00690236	Mighty Mighty Bosstones – Let's Face It	$19.95
00690040	Steve Miller Band Greatest Hits	$19.95
00694802	Gary Moore – Still Got The Blues	$19.95
00694958	Mountain, Best Of	$19.95
00690448	MxPx – The Ever Passing Moment	$19.95
00694913	Nirvana – In Utero	$19.95
00694883	Nirvana – Nevermind	$19.95
00690026	Nirvana – Acoustic In New York	$19.95
00690121	Oasis – (What's The Story) Morning Glory	$19.95
00690204	Offspring, The – Ixnay on the Hombre	$17.95
00690203	Offspring, The – Smash	$17.95
00694830	Ozzy Osbourne – No More Tears	$19.95
00694855	Pearl Jam – Ten	$19.95
00690053	Liz Phair – Whip Smart	$19.95
00690176	Phish – Billy Breathes	$22.95
00690424	Phish – Farmhouse	$19.95
00690331	Phish – The Story of Ghost	$19.95
00690428	Pink Floyd – Dark Side of the Moon	$19.95
00693800	Pink Floyd – Early Classics	$19.95
00690456	P.O.D. – The Fundamental Elements of Southtown	$19.95
00694967	Police – Message In A Box Boxed Set	$70.00
00694974	Queen – A Night At The Opera	$19.95
00690395	Rage Against The Machine – The Battle of Los Angeles	$19.95
00690145	Rage Against The Machine – Evil Empire	$19.95
00690179	Rancid – And Out Come the Wolves	$22.95
00690055	Red Hot Chili Peppers – Bloodsugarsexmagik	$19.95
00690379	Red Hot Chili Peppers – Californication	$19.95
00690090	Red Hot Chili Peppers – One Hot Minute	$22.95
00694937	Jimmy Reed – Master Bluesman	$19.95
00694899	R.E.M. – Automatic For The People	$19.95
00690260	Jimmie Rodgers Guitar Collection	$19.95
00690014	Rolling Stones – Exile On Main Street	$24.95
00690186	Rolling Stones – Rock & Roll Circus	$19.95
00690135	Otis Rush Collection	$19.95
00690031	Santana's Greatest Hits	$19.95
00690150	Son Seals – Bad Axe Blues	$17.95
00690128	Seven Mary Three – American Standards	$19.95
00120105	Kenny Wayne Shepherd – Ledbetter Heights	$19.95
00120123	Kenny Wayne Shepherd – Trouble Is	$19.95
00690196	Silverchair – Freak Show	$19.95
00690130	Silverchair – Frogstomp	$19.95
00690041	Smithereens – Best Of	$19.95
00690385	Sonicflood	$19.95
00694885	Spin Doctors – Pocket Full Of Kryptonite	$19.95
00694921	Steppenwolf, The Best Of	$22.95
00694957	Rod Stewart – Acoustic Live	$22.95
00690021	Sting – Fields Of Gold	$19.95
00690242	Suede – Coming Up	$19.95
00694824	Best Of James Taylor	$16.95
00690238	Third Eye Blind	$19.95
00690403	Third Eye Blind – Blue	$19.95
00690267	311	$19.95
00690030	Toad The Wet Sprocket	$19.95
00690228	Tonic – Lemon Parade	$19.95
00690295	Tool – Aenima	$19.95
00690039	Steve Vai – Alien Love Secrets	$24.95
00690172	Steve Vai – Fire Garden	$24.95
00690023	Jimmie Vaughan – Strange Pleasures	$19.95
00690370	Stevie Ray Vaughan and Double Trouble – The Real Deal: Greatest Hits Volume 2	$22.95
00690455	Stevie Ray Vaughan – Blues at Sunrise	$19.95
00660136	Stevie Ray Vaughan – In Step	$19.95
00690417	Stevie Ray Vaughan – Live at Carnegie Hall	$19.95
00694835	Stevie Ray Vaughan – The Sky Is Crying	$19.95
00694776	Vaughan Brothers – Family Style	$19.95
00120026	Joe Walsh – Look What I Did...	$24.95
00694789	Muddy Waters – Deep Blues	$24.95
00690071	Weezer	$19.95
00690286	Weezer – Pinkerton	$19.95
00690447	Who, The – Best of	$24.95
00694971	Who, The – Definitive Collection A-E	$24.95
00694972	Who, The – Definitive Collection F-Li	$24.95
00694972	Who, The – Definitive Collection Lo-R	$24.95
00694973	Who, The – Definitive Collection S-Y	$24.95
00690319	Stevie Wonder Hits	$17.95

Prices and availability subject to change without notice.
Some products may not be available outside the U.S.A.

FOR A COMPLETE LIST OF GUITAR RECORDED VERSIONS TITLES, SEE YOUR LOCAL MUSIC DEALER, OR WRITE TO:

HAL•LEONARD® CORPORATION
7777 W. BLUEMOUND RD. P.O. BOX 13819 MILWAUKEE, WI 53213

Visit Hal Leonard online at www.halleonard.com

0401

RECORDED VERSIONS
THE BEST NOTE-FOR-NOTE TRANSCRIPTIONS AVAILABLE!

All Guitar and Bass Books Include Tablature

RECORDED VERSIONS FOR GUITAR

00692015	Aerosmith's Greatest Hits	$18.95
00660133	Aerosmith – Pump	$18.95
00660225	Alice In Chains – Facelift	$18.95
00694826	Anthrax – Attack Of The Killer B's	$18.95
00660227	Anthrax – Persistence Of Time	$18.95
00694797	Armored Saint – Symbol Of Salvation	$18.95
00660051	Badlands	$18.95
00694863	Beatles – Sgt. Pepper's Lonely Hearts Club Band	$18.95
00694832	Beatles – Acoustic Guitar Book	$16.95
00660140	The Beatles Guitar Book	$18.95
00699041	The Best of George Benson	$18.95
00692385	Chuck Berry	$18.95
00692200	Black Sabbath – We Sold Our Soul For Rock 'N' Roll	$18.95
00694770	Jon Bon Jovi – Blaze Of Glory	$18.95
00694774	Bon Jovi – New Jersey	$18.95
00694775	Bon Jovi – Slippery When Wet	$18.95
00694762	Cinderella – Heartbreak Station	$18.95
00692376	Cinderella – Long Cold Winter	$18.95
00692375	Cinderella – Night Songs	$18.95
00694869	Eric Clapton – Unplugged	$18.95
00692392	Eric Clapton – Crossroads Vol. 1	$22.95
00692393	Eric Clapton – Crossroads Vol. 2	$22.95
00692394	Eric Clapton – Crossroads Vol. 3	$22.95
00660139	Eric Clapton – Journeyman	$18.95
00692391	The Best of Eric Clapton	$18.95
00694873	Eric Clapton – Time Pieces	$24.95
00694788	Classic Rock	$17.95
00694793	Classic Rock Instrumentals	$16.95
00694862	Contemporary Country Guitar	$17.95
00660127	Alice Cooper – Trash	$18.95
00694840	Cream – Disraeli Gears	$14.95
00694844	Def Leppard – Adrenalize	$18.95
00692440	Def Leppard – High 'N' Dry/Pyromania	$18.95
00692430	Def Leppard – Hysteria	$18.95
00660186	Alex De Grassi Guitar Collection	$16.95
00694831	Derek And The Dominos – Layla & Other Assorted Love Songs	$19.95
00692240	Bo Diddley Guitar Solos	$18.95
00660175	Dio – Lock Up The Wolves	$18.95
00660178	Willie Dixon	$24.95
00694800	FireHouse	$18.95
00660184	Lita Ford – Stiletto	$18.95
00694807	Danny Gatton – 88 Elmira St.	$17.95
00694848	Genuine Rockabilly Guitar Hits	$19.95
00694798	George Harrison Anthology	$19.95
00660326	Guitar Heroes	$17.95
00694780	Guitar School Classics	$17.95
00694768	Guitar School Greatest Hits	$17.95
00660325	The Harder Edge	$17.95
00692930	Jimi Hendrix-Are You Experienced?	$19.95
00692931	Jimi Hendrix-Axis: Bold As Love	$19.95
00660192	The Jimi Hendrix Concerts	$24.95
00692932	Jimi Hendrix-Electric Ladyland	$24.95
00660099	Jimi Hendrix-Radio One	$24.95
00660024	Jimi Hendrix-Variations On A Theme: Red House	$18.95
00660029	Buddy Holly	$18.95
00660200	John Lee Hooker – The Healer	$18.95
00660169	John Lee Hooker – A Blues Legend	$17.95
00694850	Iron Maiden – Fear Of The Dark	$19.95
00694761	Iron Maiden – No Prayer For The Dying	$18.95
00693097	Iron Maiden – Seventh Son Of A Seventh Son	$18.95
00693096	Iron Maiden – Power Slave/Somewhere In Time	$19.95
00693095	Iron Maiden	$22.95
00694833	Billy Joel For Guitar	$18.95
00660147	Eric Johnson Guitar Transcriptions	$18.95
00694799	Robert Johnson – At The Crossroads	$19.95
00660226	Judas Priest – Painkiller	$18.95
00693185	Judas Priest – Vintage Hits	$18.95
00693186	Judas Priest – Metal Cuts	$18.95
00693187	Judas Priest – Ram It Down	$18.95
00694764	Kentucky Headhunters – Pickin' On Nashville	$18.95
00694795	Kentucky Headhunters – Electric Barnyard	$18.95
00660050	B. B. King	$18.95
00660068	Kix – Blow My Fuse	$18.95
00694806	L.A. Guns – Hollywood Vampires	$18.95
00694794	Best Of Los Lobos	$18.95
00660199	The Lynch Mob – Wicked Sensation	$18.95
00693412	Lynyrd Skynyrd	$18.95
00660174	Yngwie Malmsteen – Eclipse	$18.95
00694845	Yngwie Malmsteen – Fire And Ice	$18.95
00694756	Yngwie Malmsteen – Marching Out	$18.95
00694755	Yngwie Malmsteen's Rising Force	$18.95
00660001	Yngwie Malmsteen Rising Force – Odyssey	$18.95
00694757	Yngwie Malmsteen – Trilogy	$18.95
00692880	Metal Madness	$17.95
00694792	Metal Church – The Human Factor	$18.95
00660229	Monster Metal Ballads	$19.95
00694802	Gary Moore – Still Got The Blues	$18.95
00694872	Vinnie Moore – Meltdown	$18.95
00693495	Vinnie Moore – Time Odyssey	$18.95
00694830	Ozzy Osbourne – No More Tears	$18.95
00694855	Pearl Jam – Ten	$18.95
00693800	Pink Floyd – Early Classics	$18.95
00660188	Poison – Flesh & Blood	$18.95
00693866	Poison – Open Up & Say...AHH	$18.95
00693865	Poison – Look What The Cat Dragged In	$18.95
00693864	The Best of Police	$18.95
00692535	Elvis Presley	$18.95
00693910	Ratt – Invasion Of Your Privacy	$18.95
00693911	Ratt – Out Of The Cellar	$18.95
00660060	Robbie Robertson	$18.95
00694760	Rock Classics	$17.95
00693474	Rock Superstars	$17.95
00694836	Richie Sambora – Stranger In This Town	$18.95
00694805	Scorpions – Crazy World	$18.95
00694796	Steelheart	$18.95
00694180	Stryper – In God We Trust	$18.95
00694824	Best Of James Taylor	$14.95
00694846	Testament – The Ritual	$18.95
00660084	Testament – Practice What You Preach	$18.95
00694765	Testament – Souls Of Black	$18.95
00694767	Trixter	$18.95
00694410	The Best of U2	$18.95
00694411	U2 – The Joshua Tree	$18.95
00660137	Steve Vai – Passion & Warfare	$24.95
00660136	Stevie Ray Vaughan – In Step	$18.95
00660058	Stevie Ray Vaughan – Lightnin' Blues 1983 – 1987	$22.95
00694835	Stevie Ray Vaughan – The Sky Is Crying	$18.95
00694776	Vaughan Brothers – Family Style	$18.95
00660196	Vixen – Rev It Up	$18.95
00660054	W.A.S.P. – The Headless Children	$18.95
00694787	Warrant – Dirty Rotten Filthy Stinking Rich	$18.95
00694781	Warrant – Cherry Pie	$18.95
00694786	Winger	$18.95
00694782	Winger – In The Heart Of The Young	$18.95

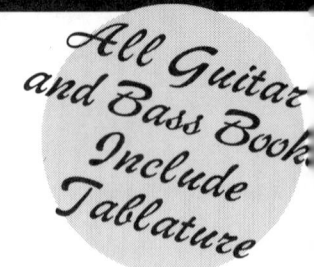

Prices and availability subject to change without notice.

For more information, see your local music dealer, or write to:

Hal Leonard Publishing Corporation
P.O. Box 13819 Milwaukee, Wisconsin 53213

EASY RECORDED VERSIONS FOR GUITAR

00660159	The Best Of Aerosmith	$14.95
00660134	Aerosmith – Pump	$14.95
00694785	Beatles Best	$14.95
00660117	Black Sabbath – We Sold Our Soul For Rock 'N' Roll	$12.95
00660094	The Best of Eric Clapton	$14.95
00699331	Early Rock Hits	$12.95
00660097	Jimi Hendrix – Are You Experienced?	$12.95
00660195	Jimi Hendrix – Axis: Bold As Love	$12.95
00660201	Jimi Hendrix – Electric Ladyland	$12.95
00660122	Lynyrd Skynyrd	$14.95
00660173	Pink Floyd- Dark Side of the Moon	$14.95
00660118	Pink Floyd – Early Classics	$12.95
00660206	The Best Of The Police	$14.95
00699332	Rock And Roll Classics	$12.95
00660107	Rock Superstars	$12.95
00660096	The Best of U2	$14.95
00694839	Unplugged – Acoustic Rock Guitar Hits	$12.95
00694784	Vaughan Brothers – Family Style	$14.95

BASS RECORDED VERSIONS

00660135	Aerosmith – Pump	$14.95
00660103	Beatles Bass Book	$14.95
00694803	Best Bass Rock Hits	$12.95
00660116	Black Sabbath – We Sold Our Soul For Rock 'N' Roll	$14.95
00694771	Jon Bon Jovi – Blaze Of Glory	$12.95
00694773	Bon Jovi – New Jersey	$14.95
00694772	Bon Jovi – Slippery When Wet	$12.95
00660187	The Best Of Eric Clapton	$14.95
00692878	Heavy Metal Bass Licks	$14.95
00660132	The Buddy Holly Bass Book	$12.95
00660130	Iron Maiden – Powerslave/Somewhere In Time	$17.95
00660106	Judas Priest – Metal Cuts	$17.95
00694758	Lynch Mob – Wicked Sensation	$16.95
00660121	Lynyrd Skynyrd Bass Book	$14.95
00660082	Yngwie Malmsteen's Rising Force	$9.95
00660119	Pink Floyd – Early Classics	$14.95
00660172	Pink Floyd – Dark Side Of The Moon	$14.95
00660207	The Best of the Police	$14.95
00660085	Rockabilly Bass Book	$14.95
00694783	Best Of U2	$18.95
00694777	Stevie Ray Vaughan – In Step	$14.95
00694778	Stevie Ray Vaughan – Lightnin' Blues 1983 – 1987	$19.95
00694779	Vaughan Brothers – Family Style	$16.95
00694763	Warrant – Dirty Rotten Filthy Stinking Rich/ Cherry Pie	$16.95
00694766	Winger – Winger/In The Heart Of The Young	$16.95

DRUM RECORDED VERSIONS

00694790	Best Of Bon Jovi	$12.95
00660181	Bonham – Disregard Of Timekeeping	$14.95
06621752	Classic Rock	$12.95
00694820	Best Of Lynyrd Skynyrd	$14.95
06621751	Power Rock	$12.95
06621749	Winger – Winger/In The Heart Of The Young	$14.95

KEYBOARD RECORDED VERSIONS

00694827	Beatles Keyboard Book	$17.95
00694828	Billy Joel Keyboard Book	$17.95
00694829	Elton John Keyboard Book	$19.95